Fairy and Fantasy 5

Grayscale Coloring Book
by Christine Karron

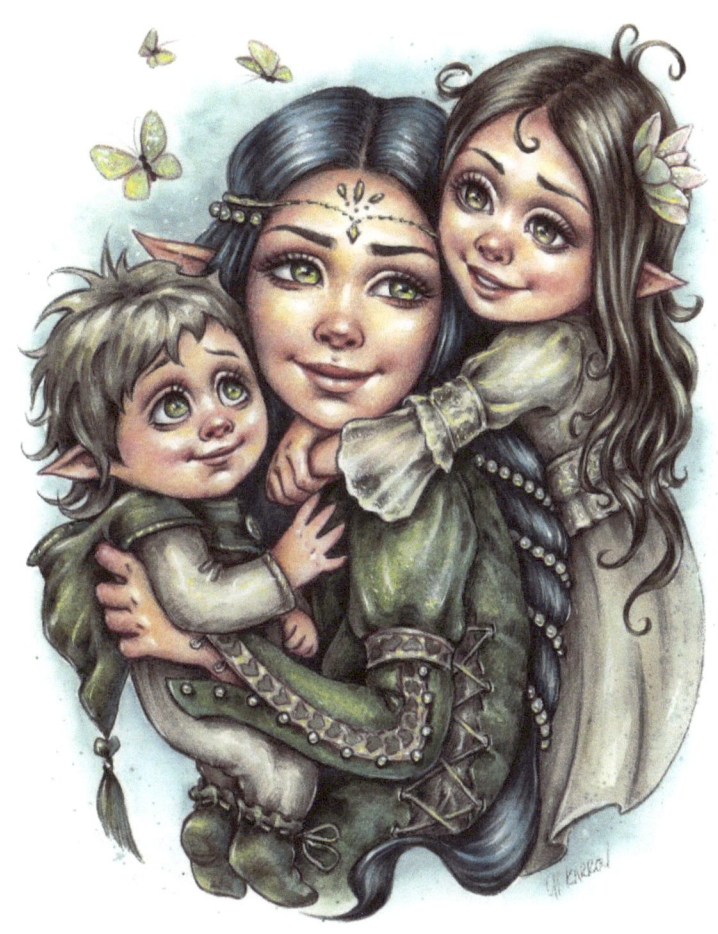

All illustrations in this book are original hand drawn pencil illustrations by the artist Christine Karron. For coloring inspirations, work-in-process videos and more about Christine's artwork visit www.chkarron.com

This coloring book is suitable for all ages and skill levels. Recommended for coloring with markers, colored pencils, pens, and crayons. If using wet media, place a sheet of thick paper or card stock behind the coloring page to prevent bleed through.

FAIRY and FANTASY 5
Grayscale Coloring book by Christine Karron

First published October 2023

ISBN: 9798865360339
Imprint: Independently published

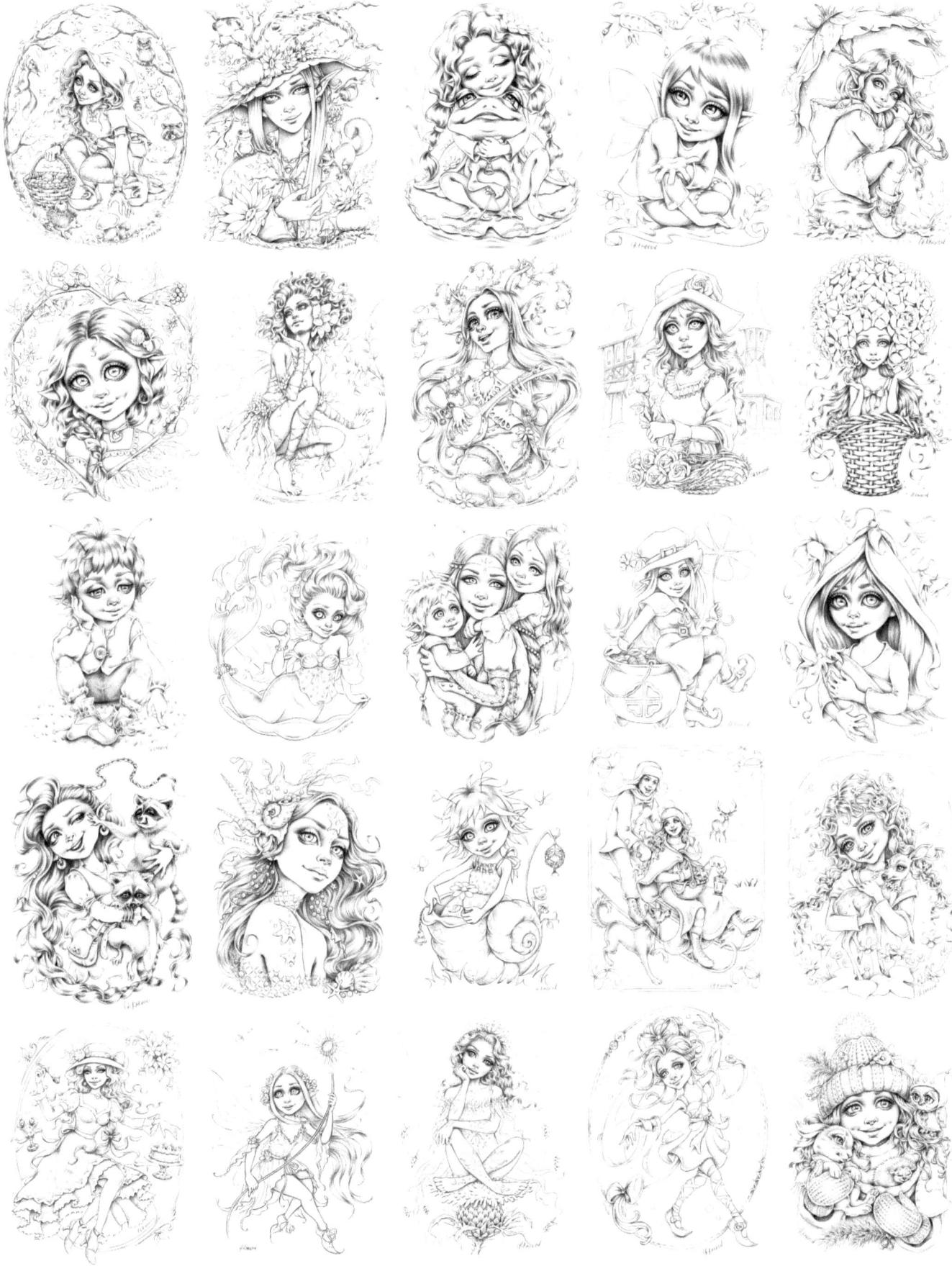

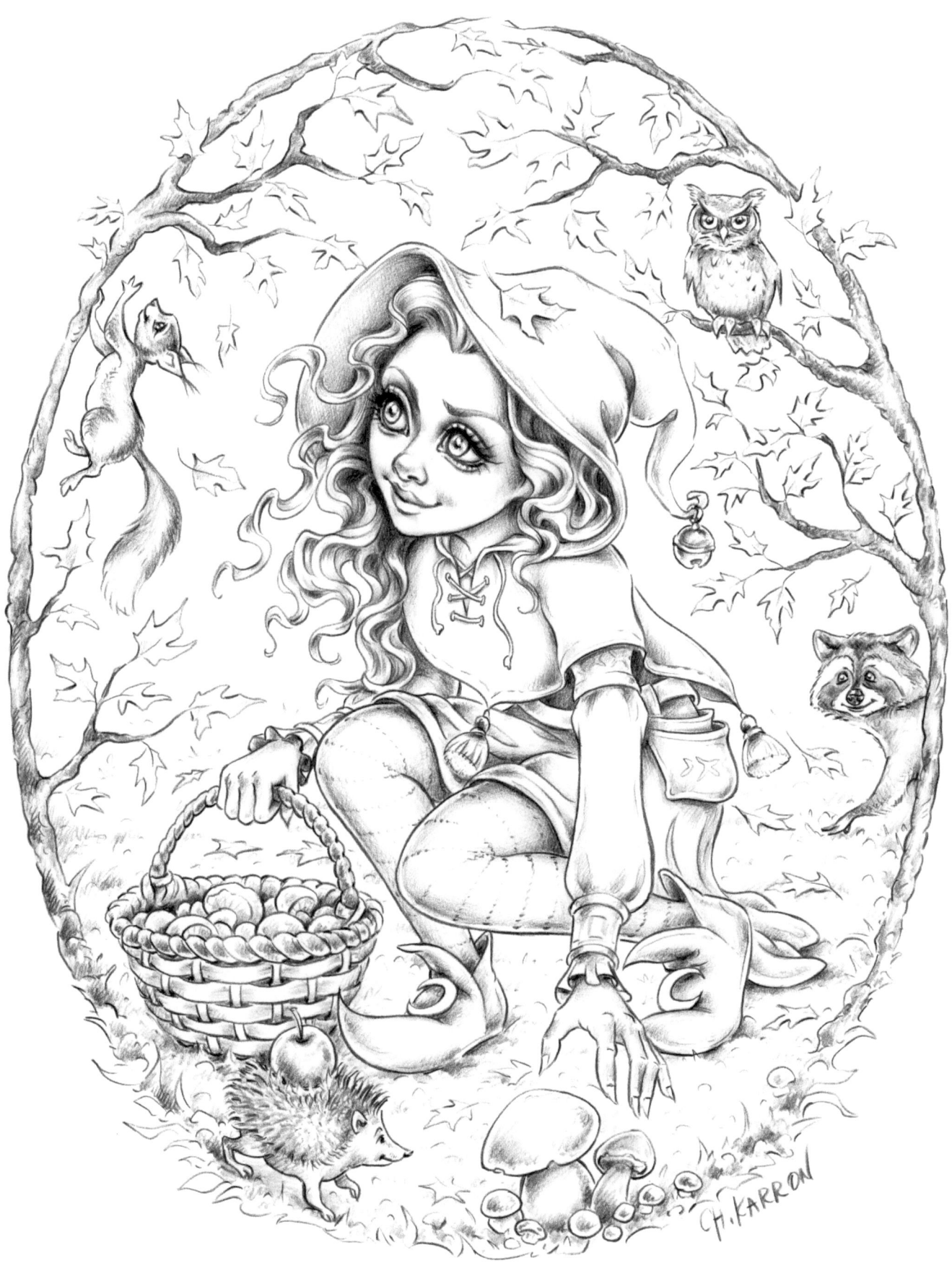

Autumn Encounters

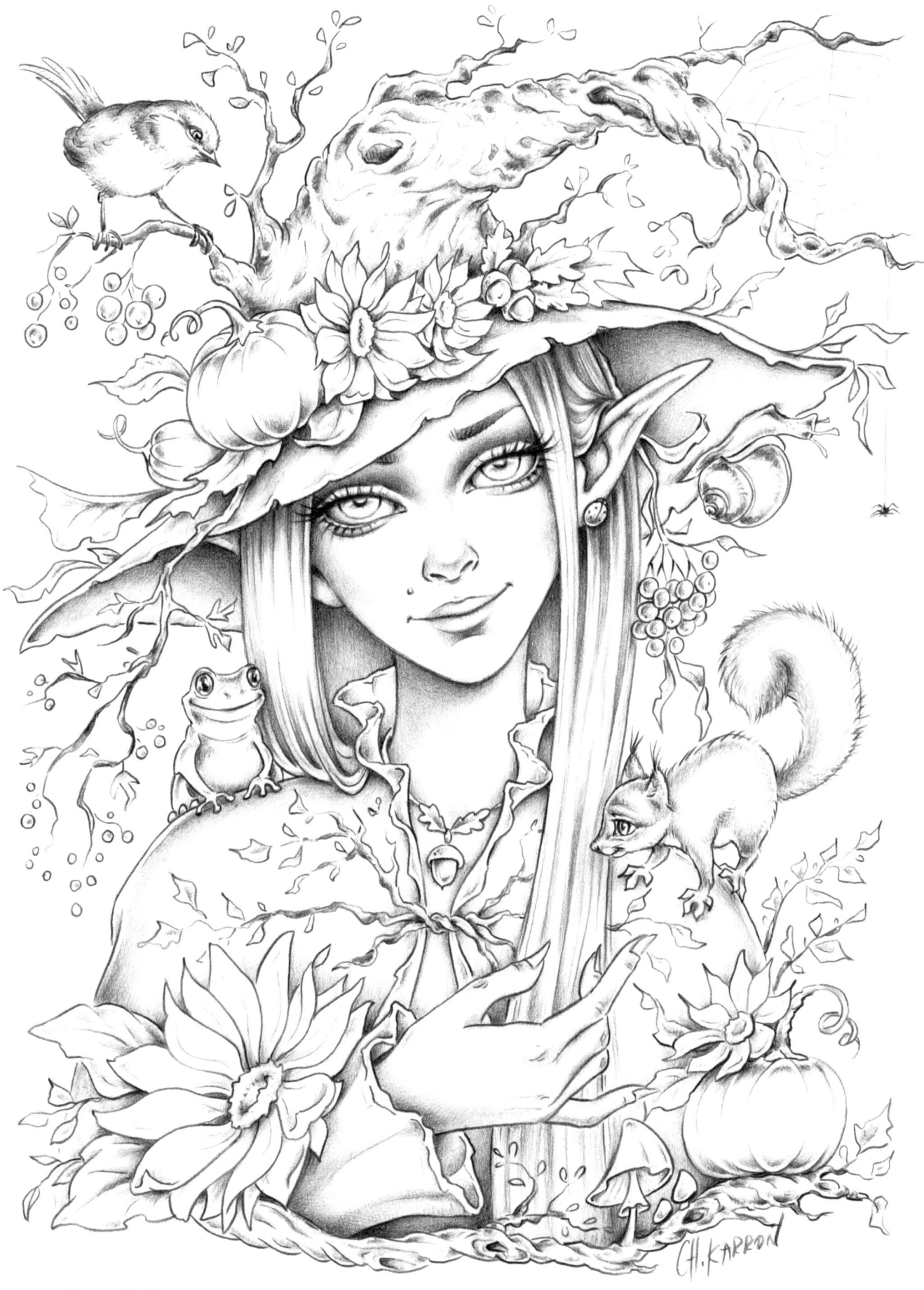

Fairy and Fantasy 5 © Christine Karron

Autumn Forest Witch

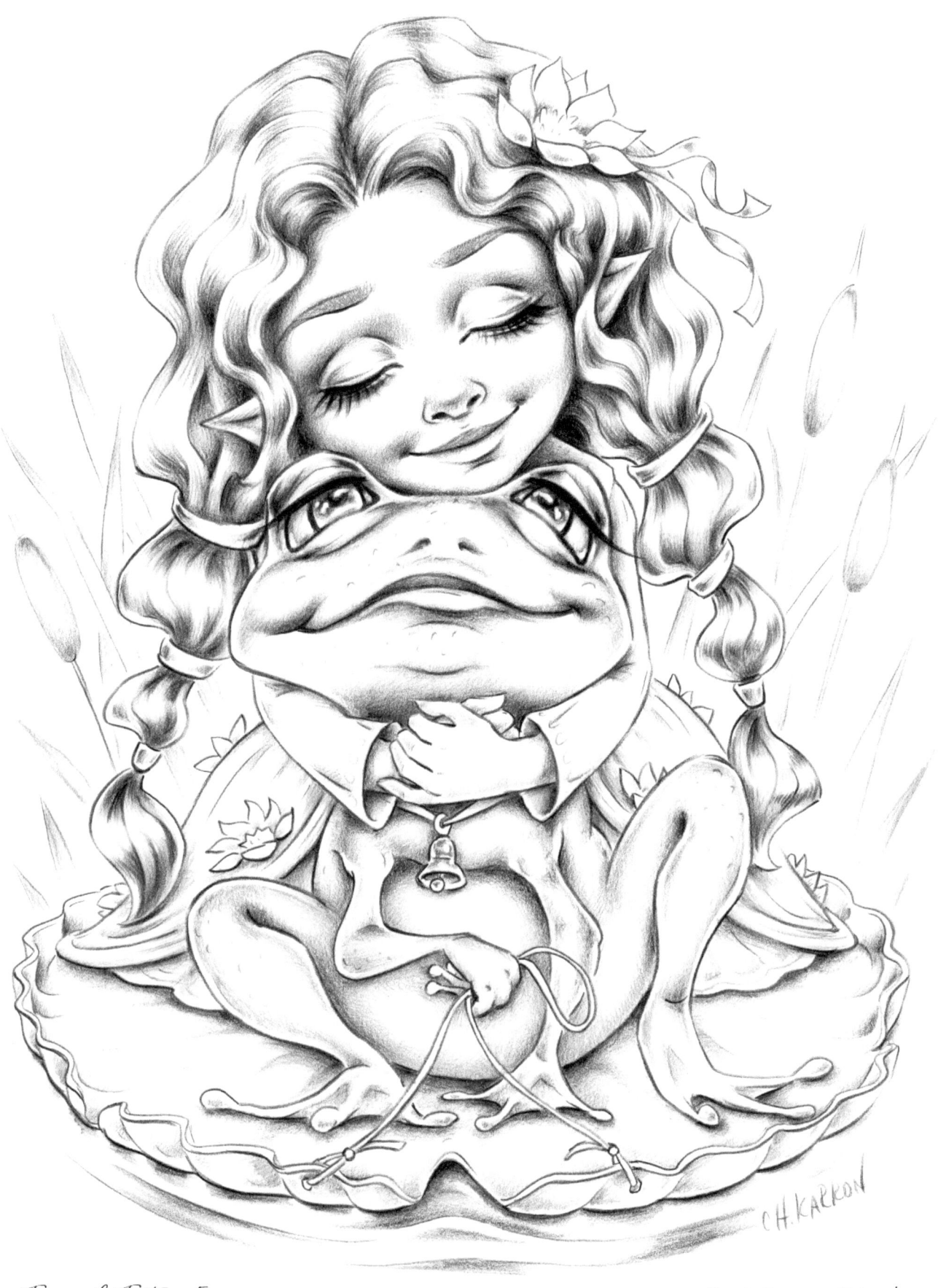

Best Froggy Friend

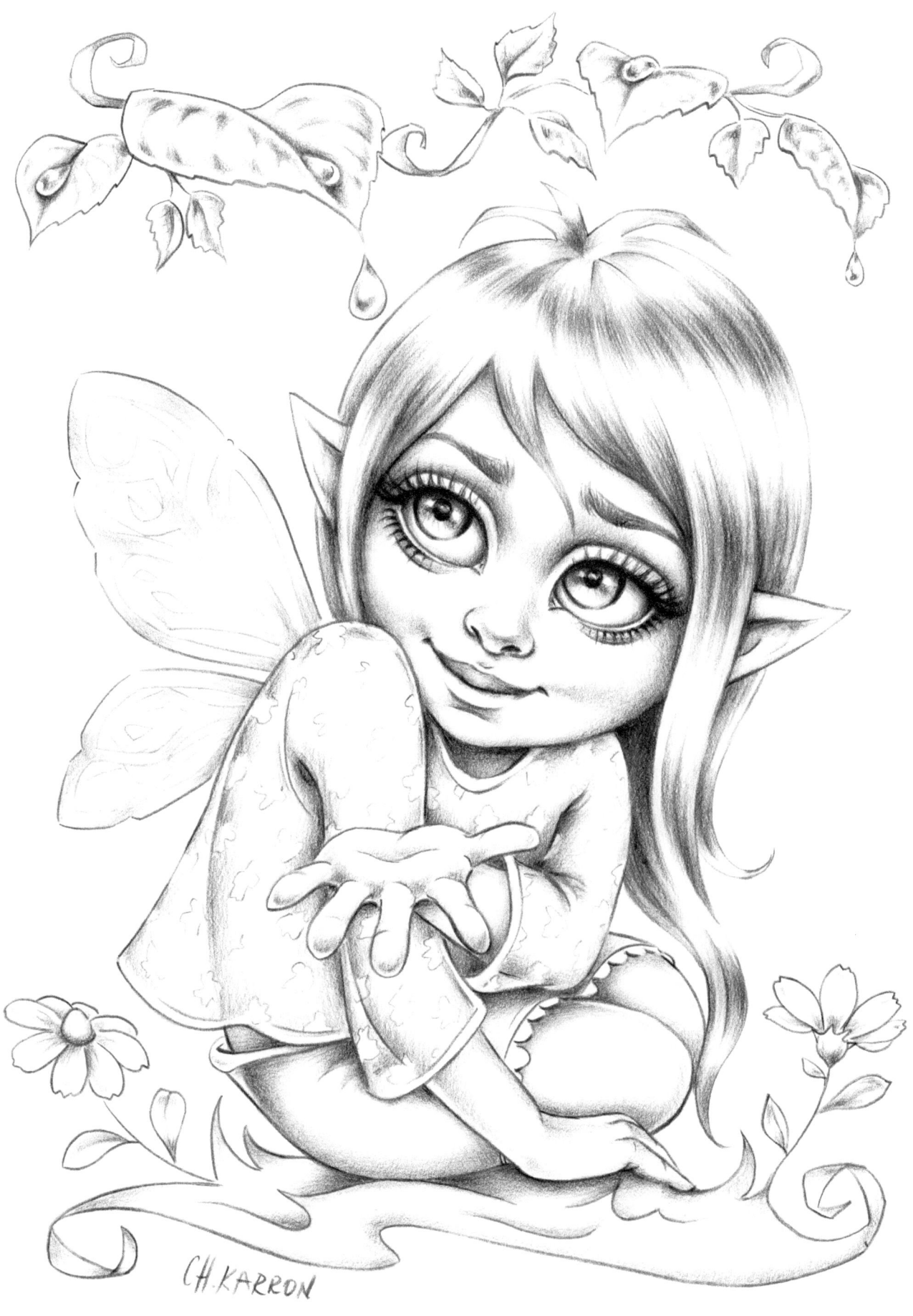

Fairy and Fantasy 5 © Christine Karron

Dew Droplet

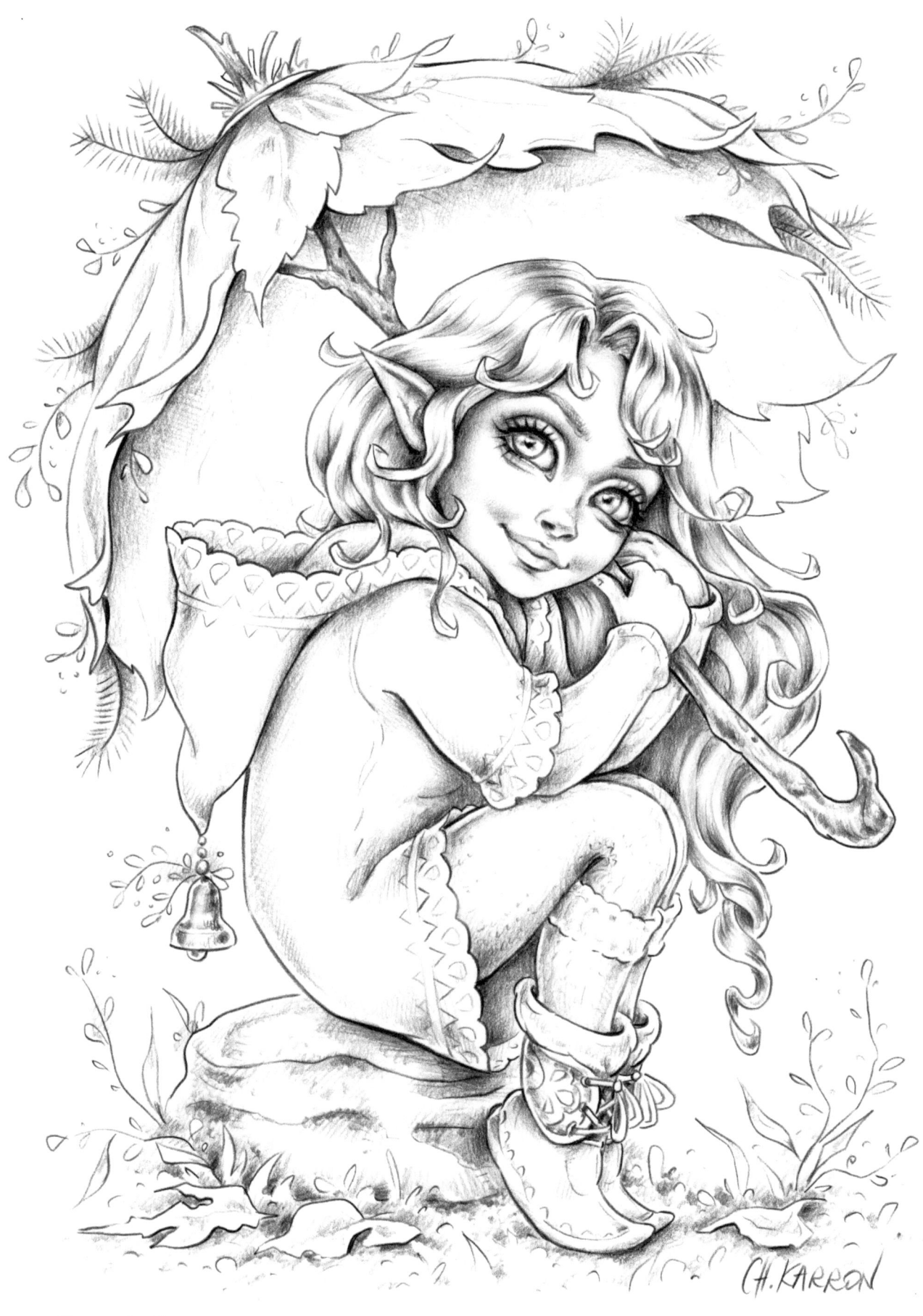

Elfling's Shelter

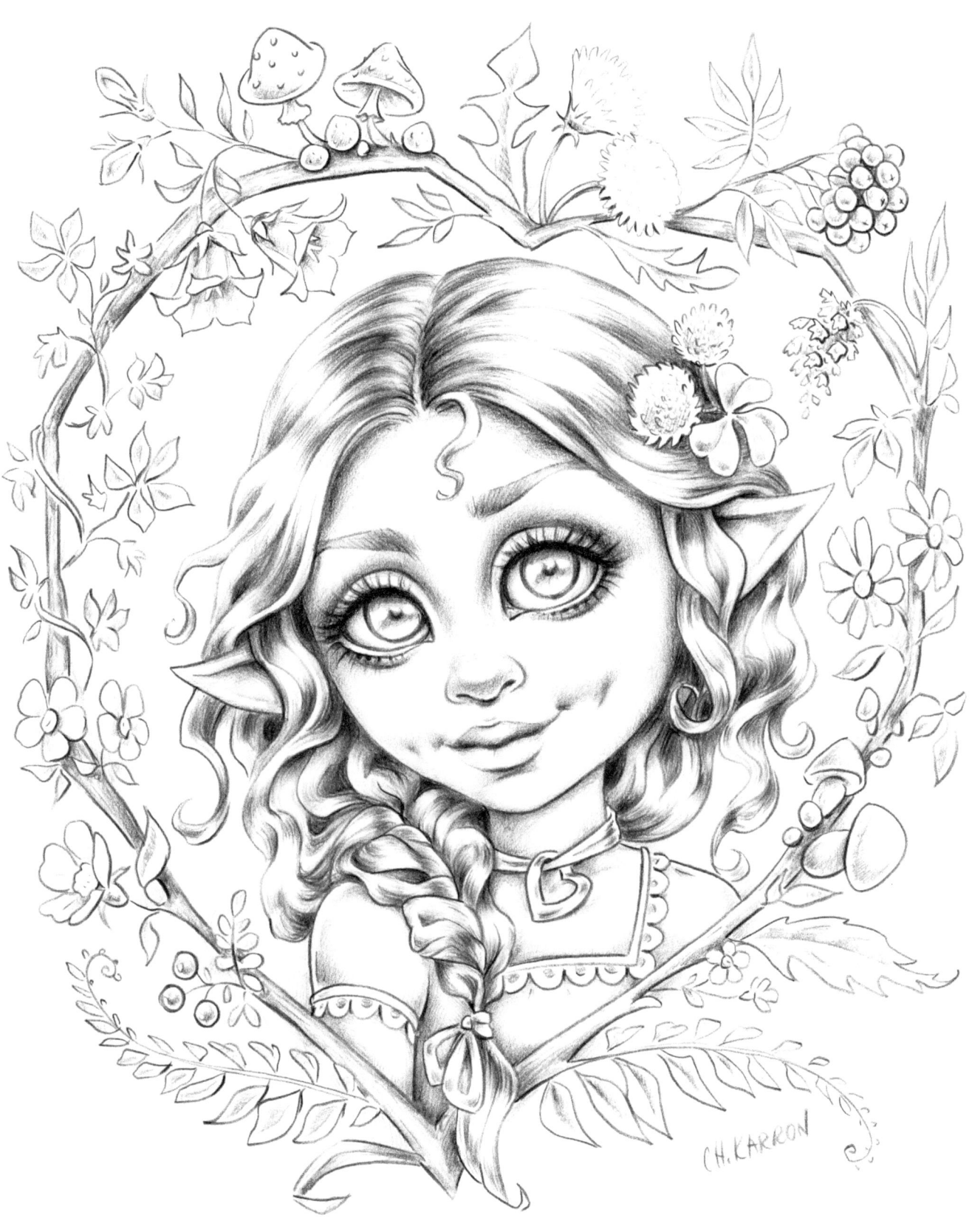

Fairy Heart

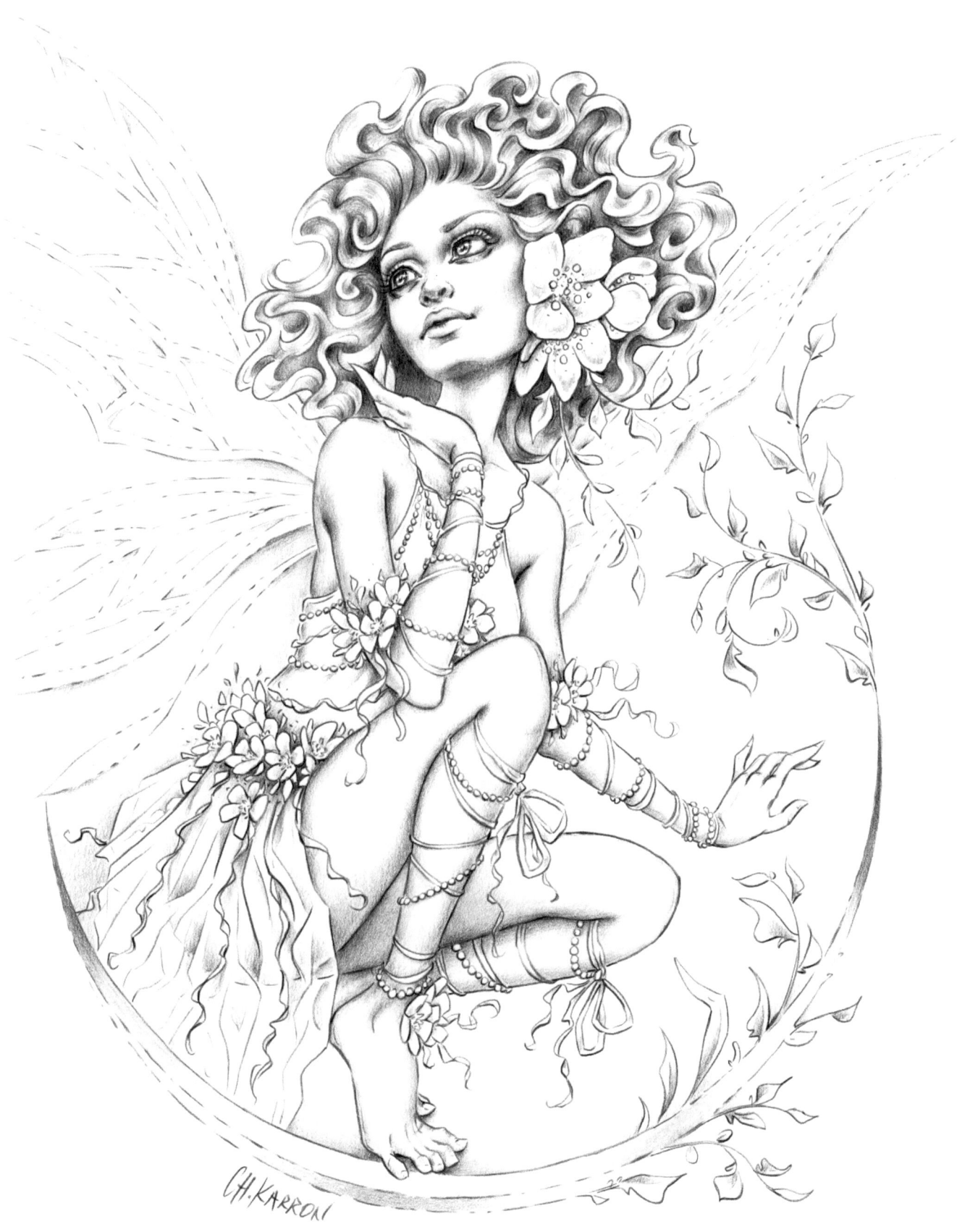

Fairy Portal

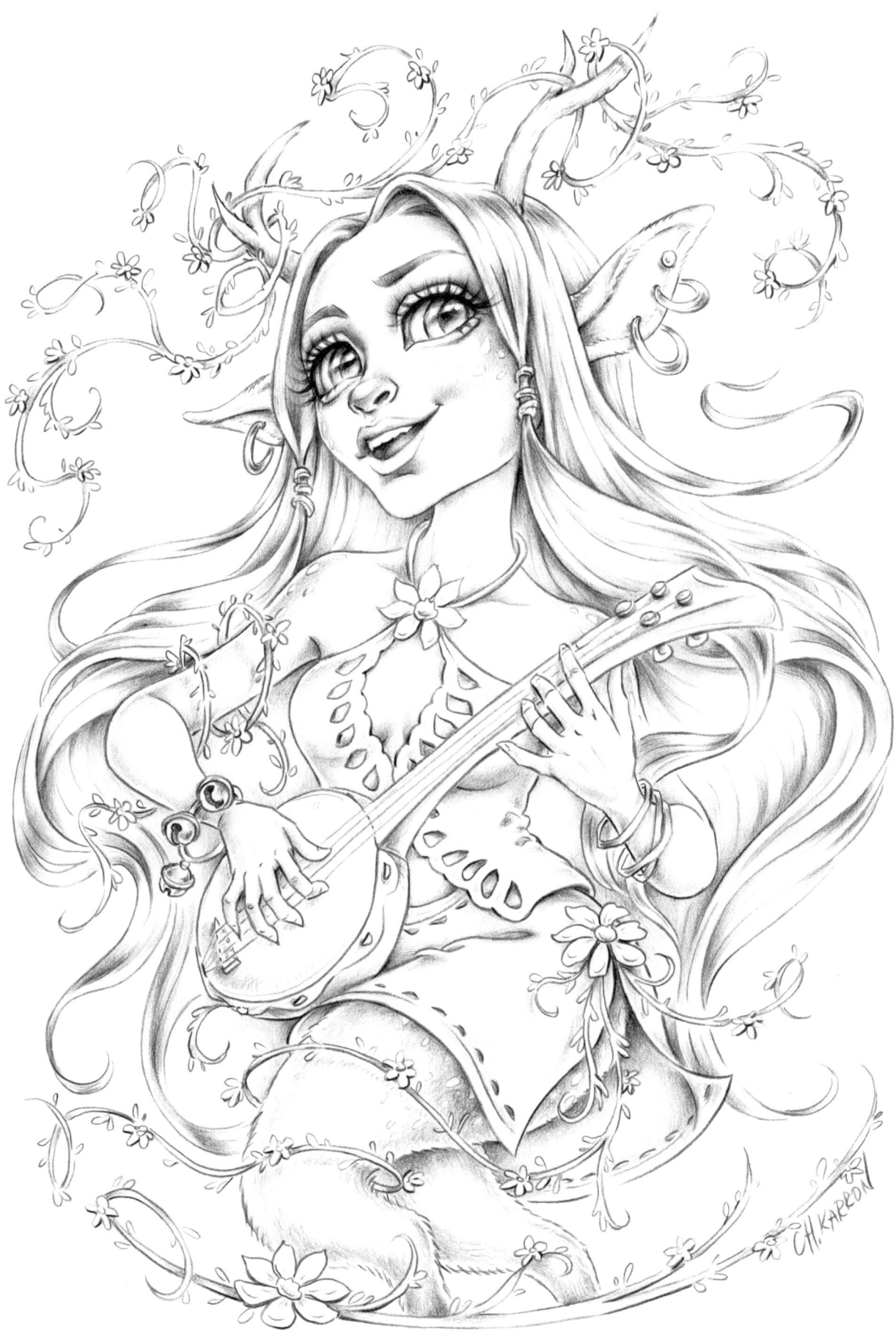

Fairy and Fantasy 5 © Christine Karron

Faun Jingle

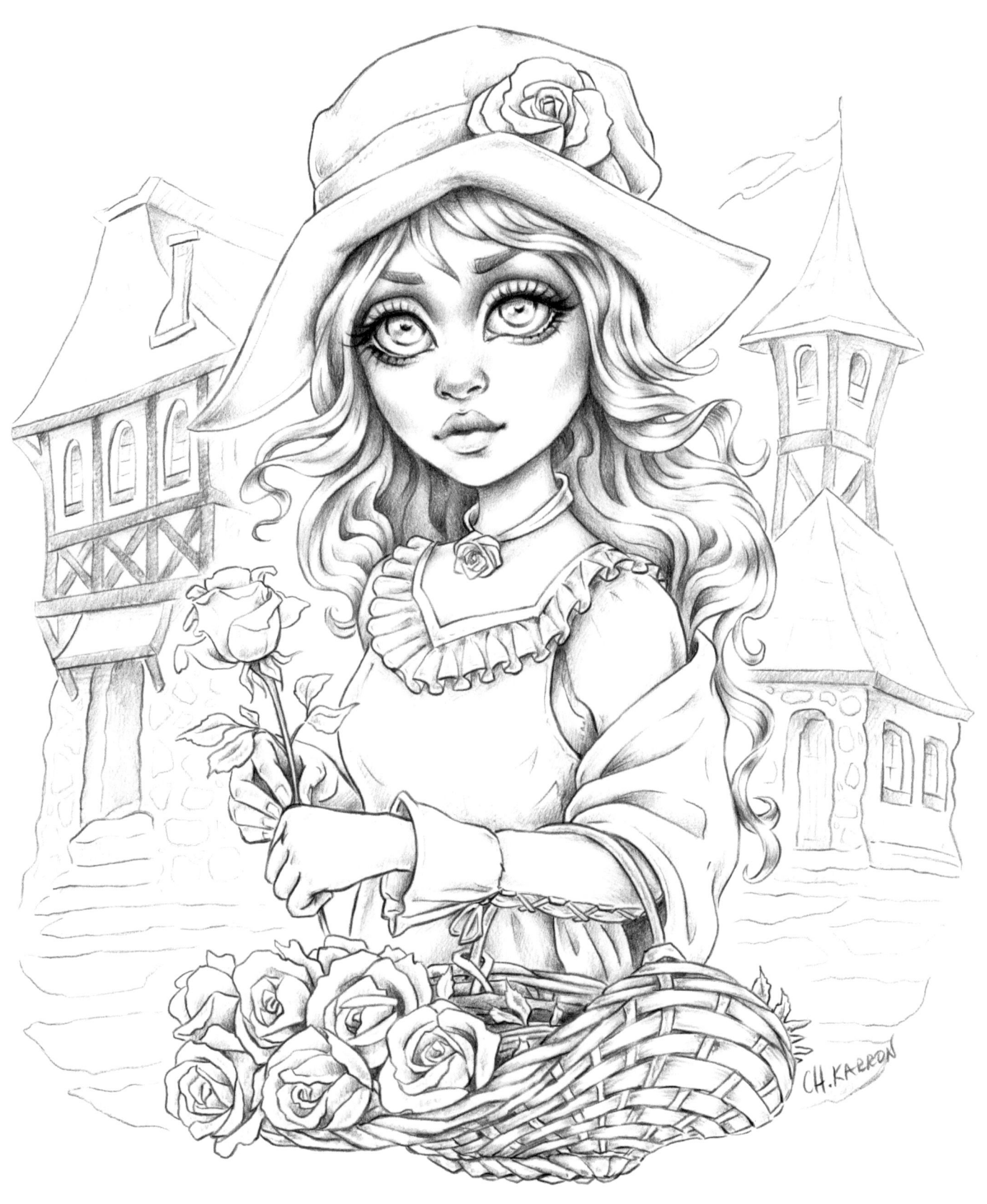

Flower Girl

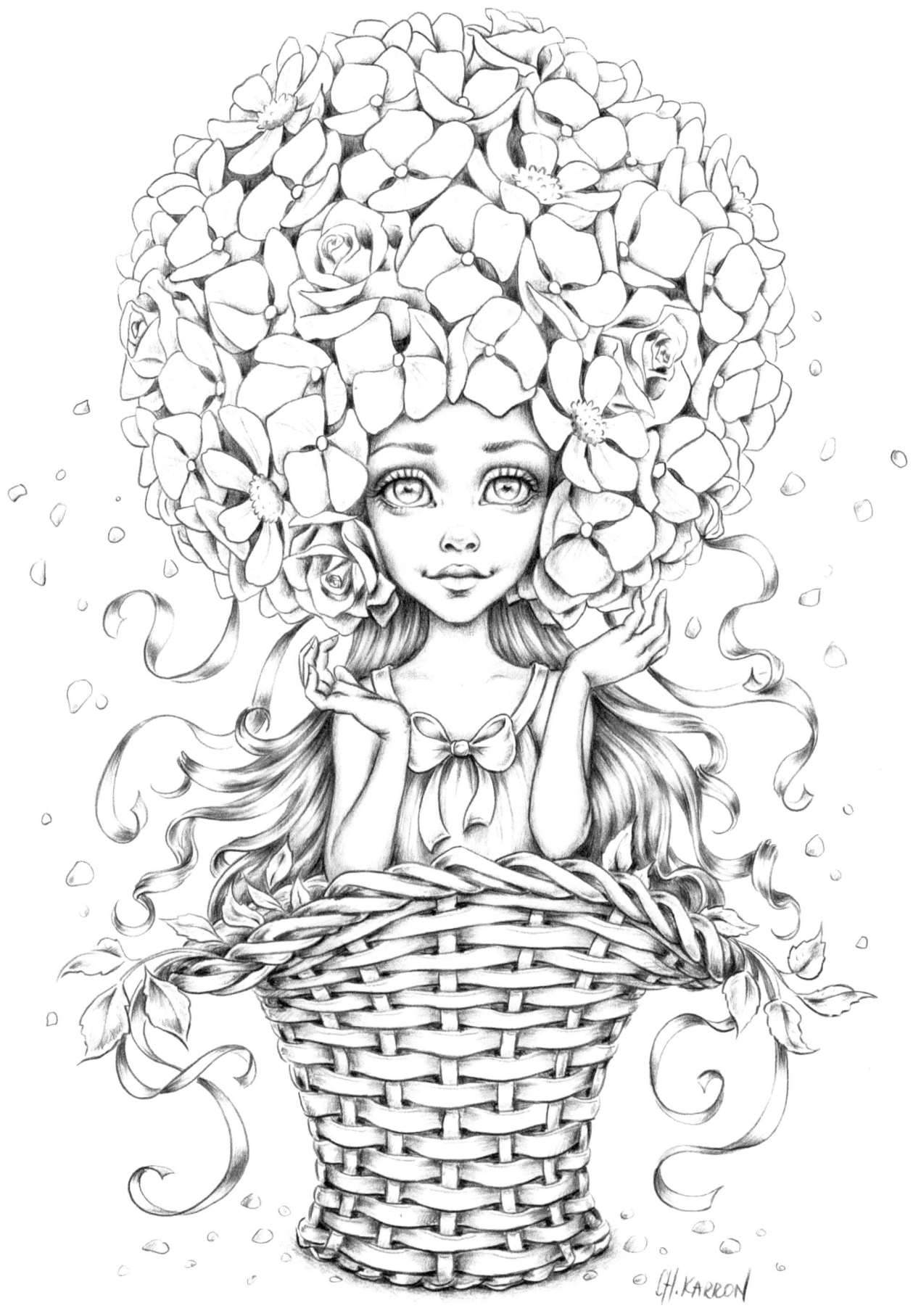

Fairy and Fantasy 5 © Christine Karron

Flowerling

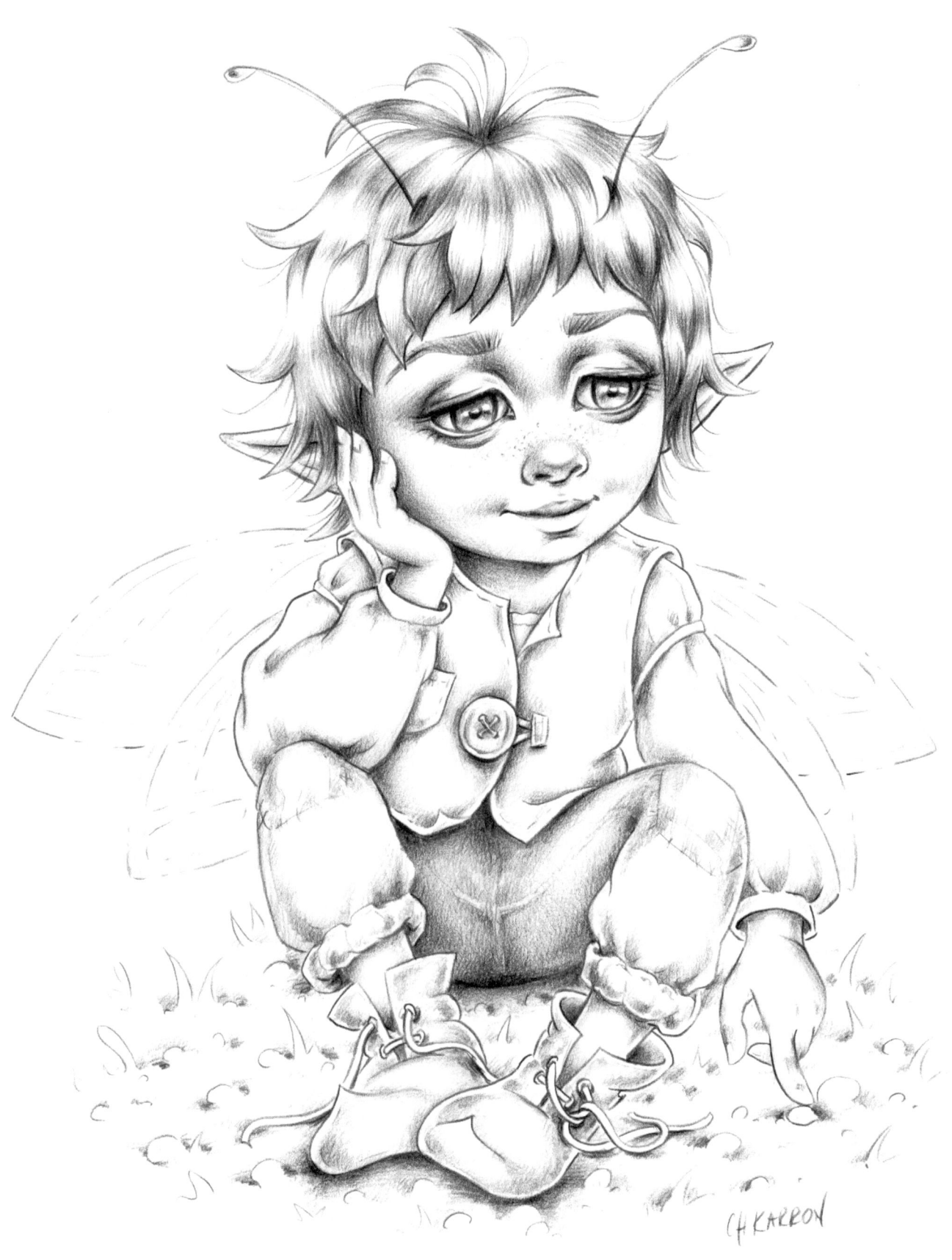

Little Fairy Boy

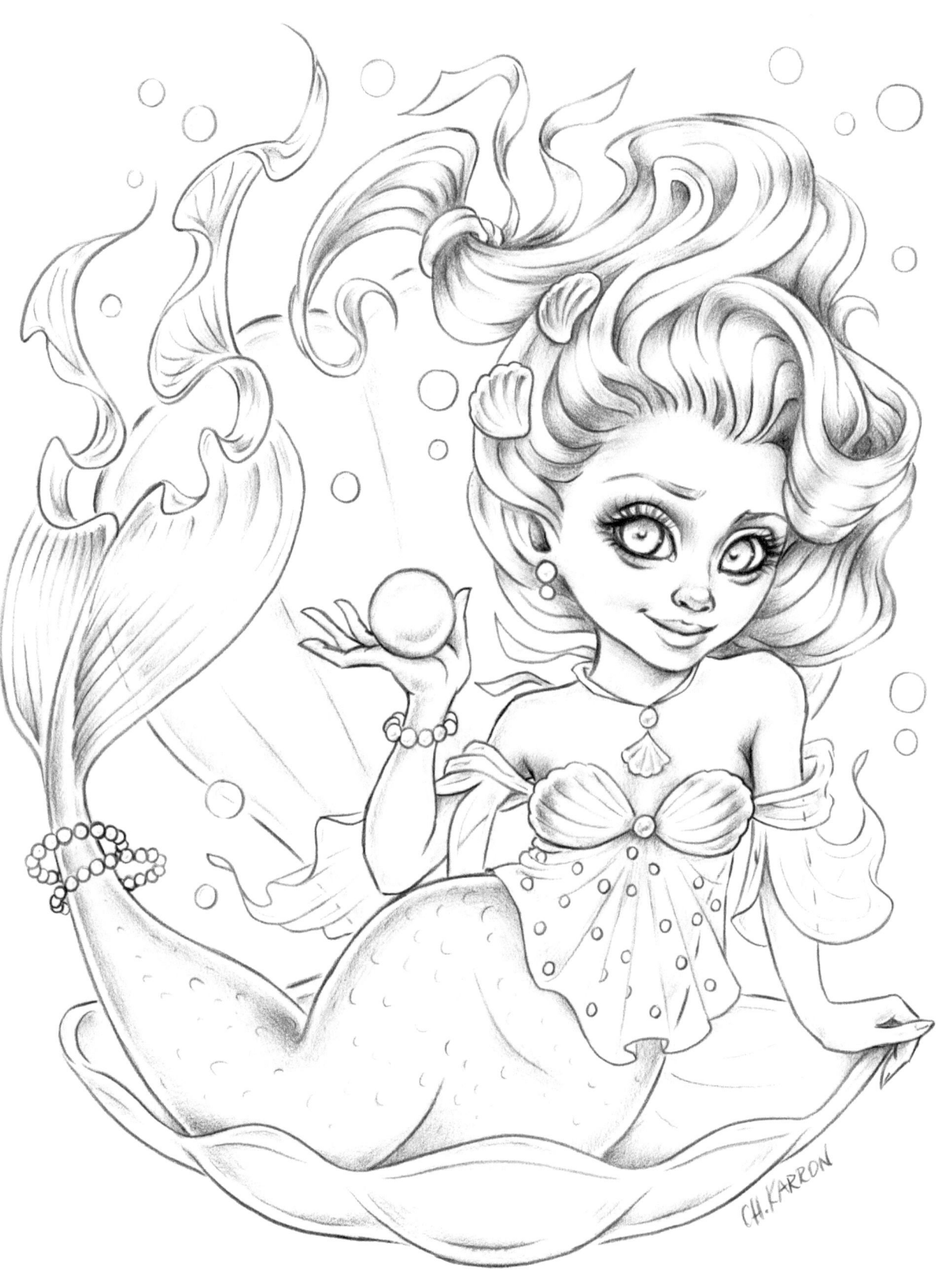

Mermaid's Pearl

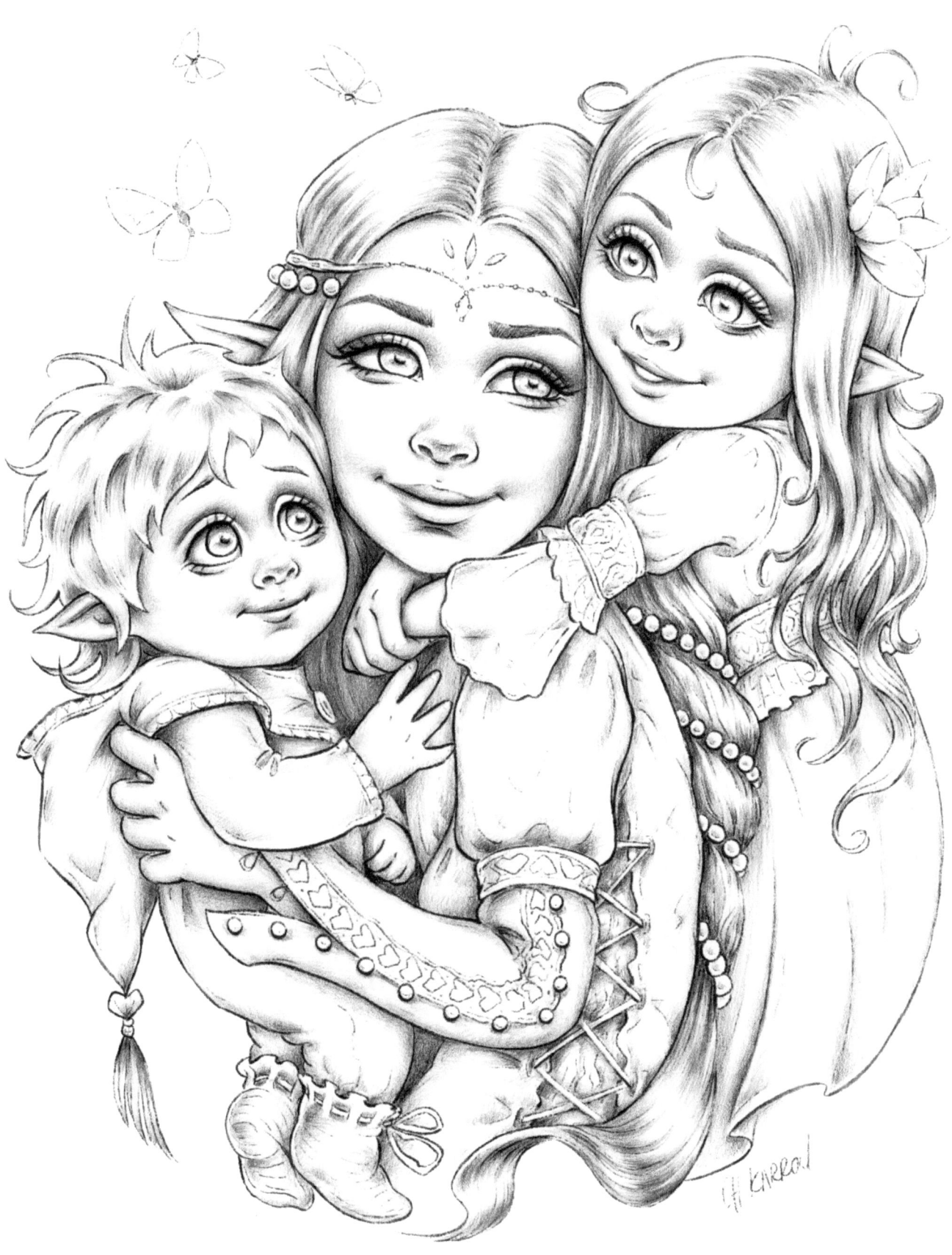

Fairy and Fantasy 5 © Christine Karron

Mother's love

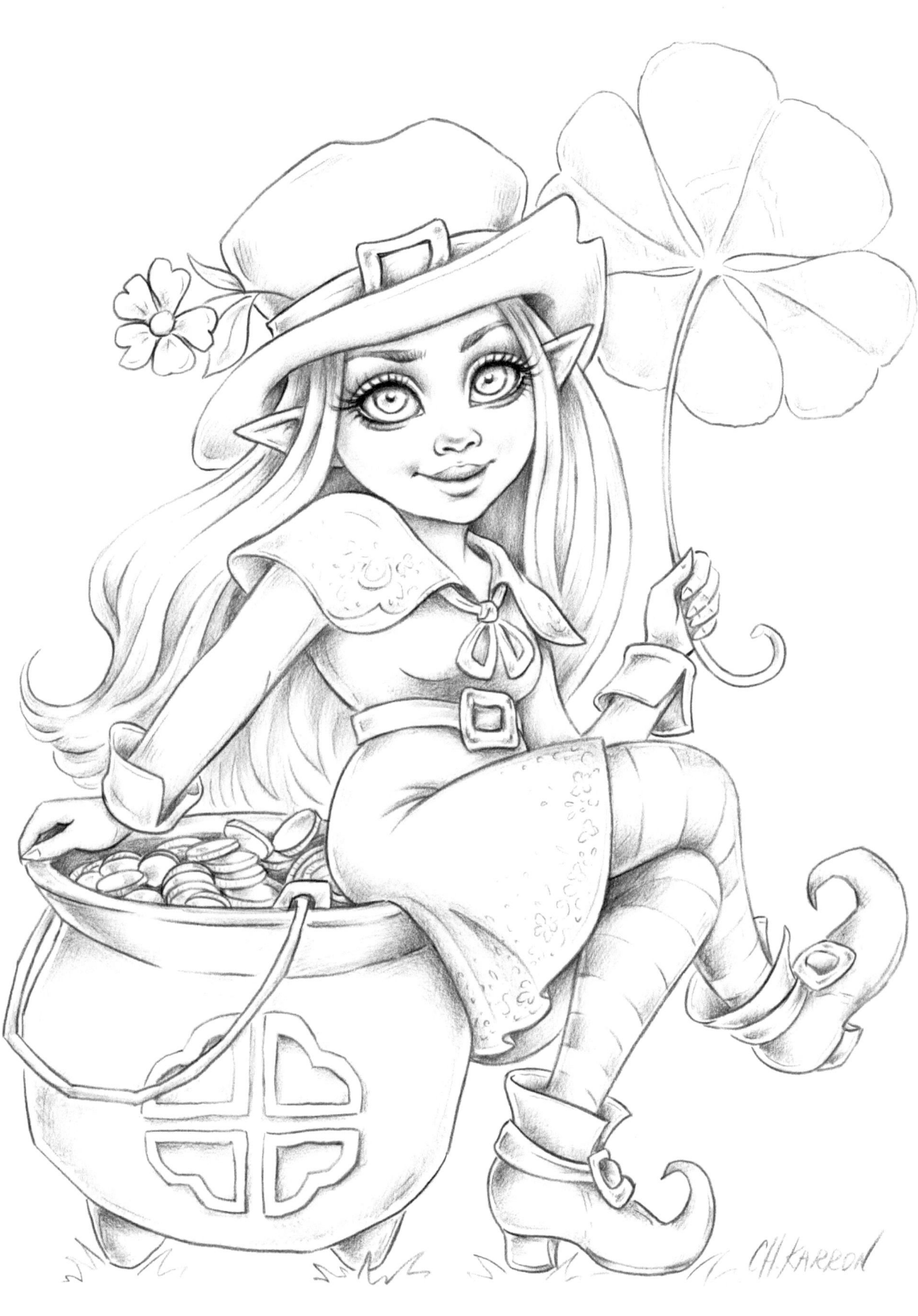

Ms Leprechaun

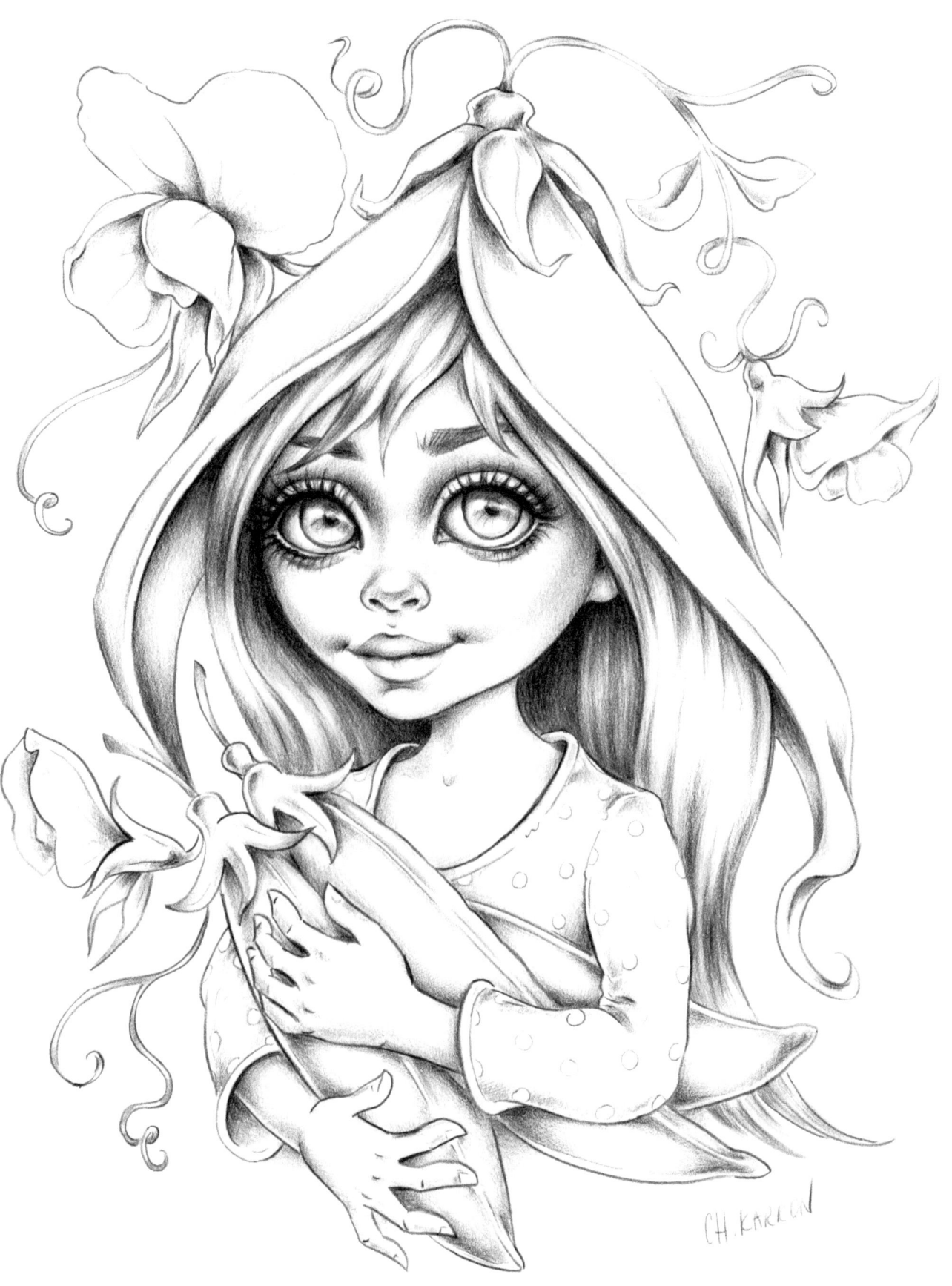

Pea Elfling

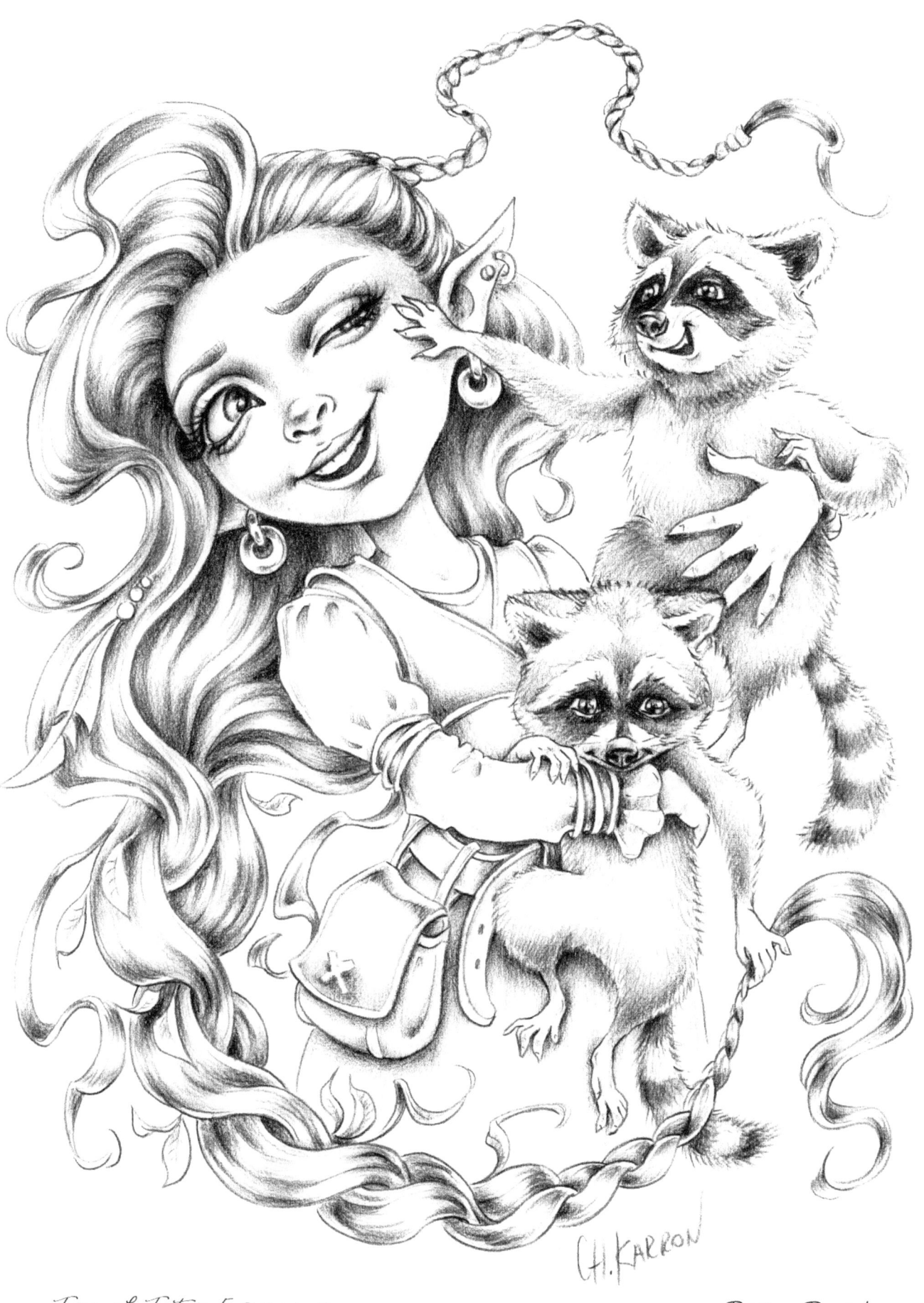

Fairy and Fantasy 5 © Christine Karron

Raccoon Rascals

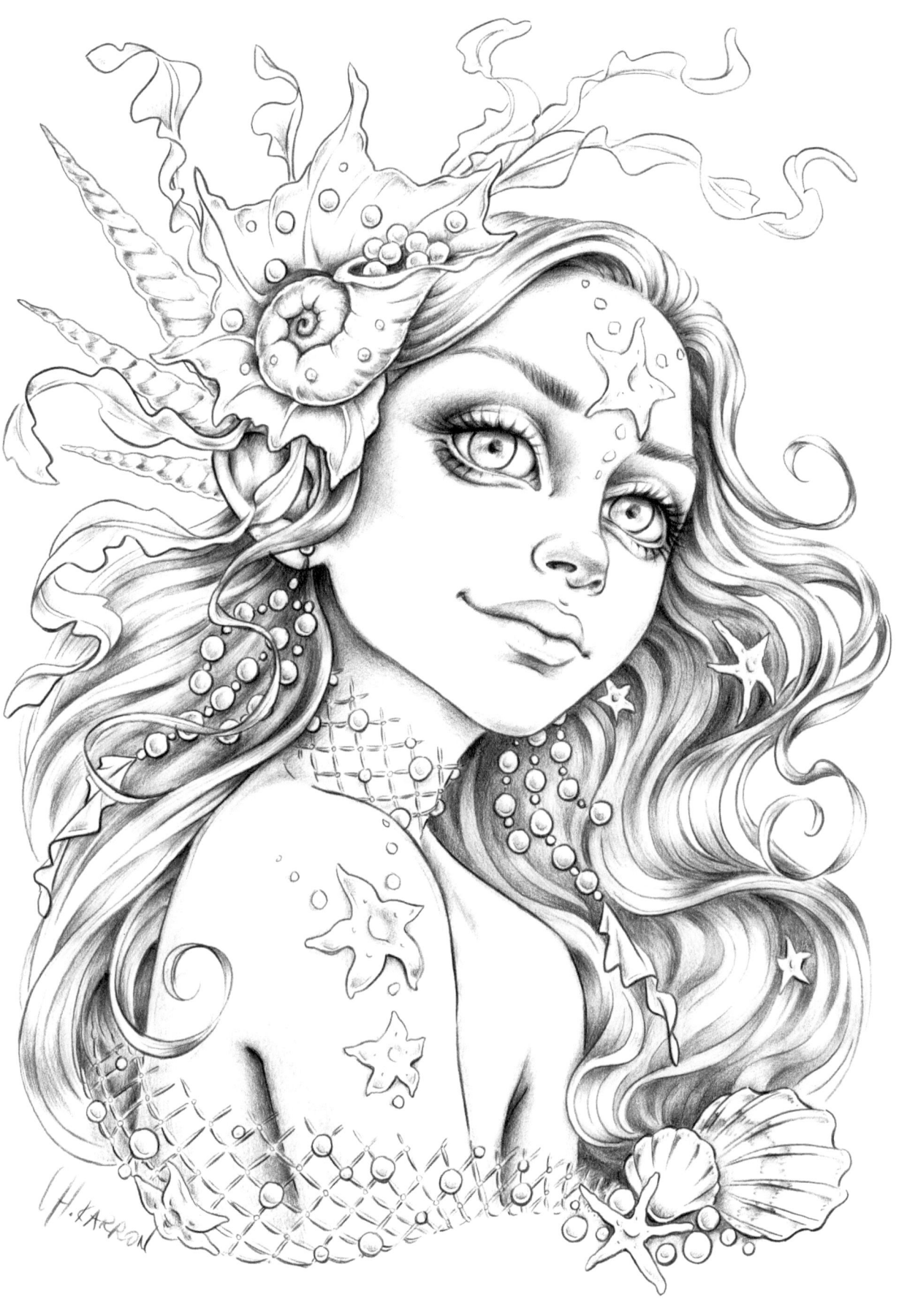

Sea Pearls

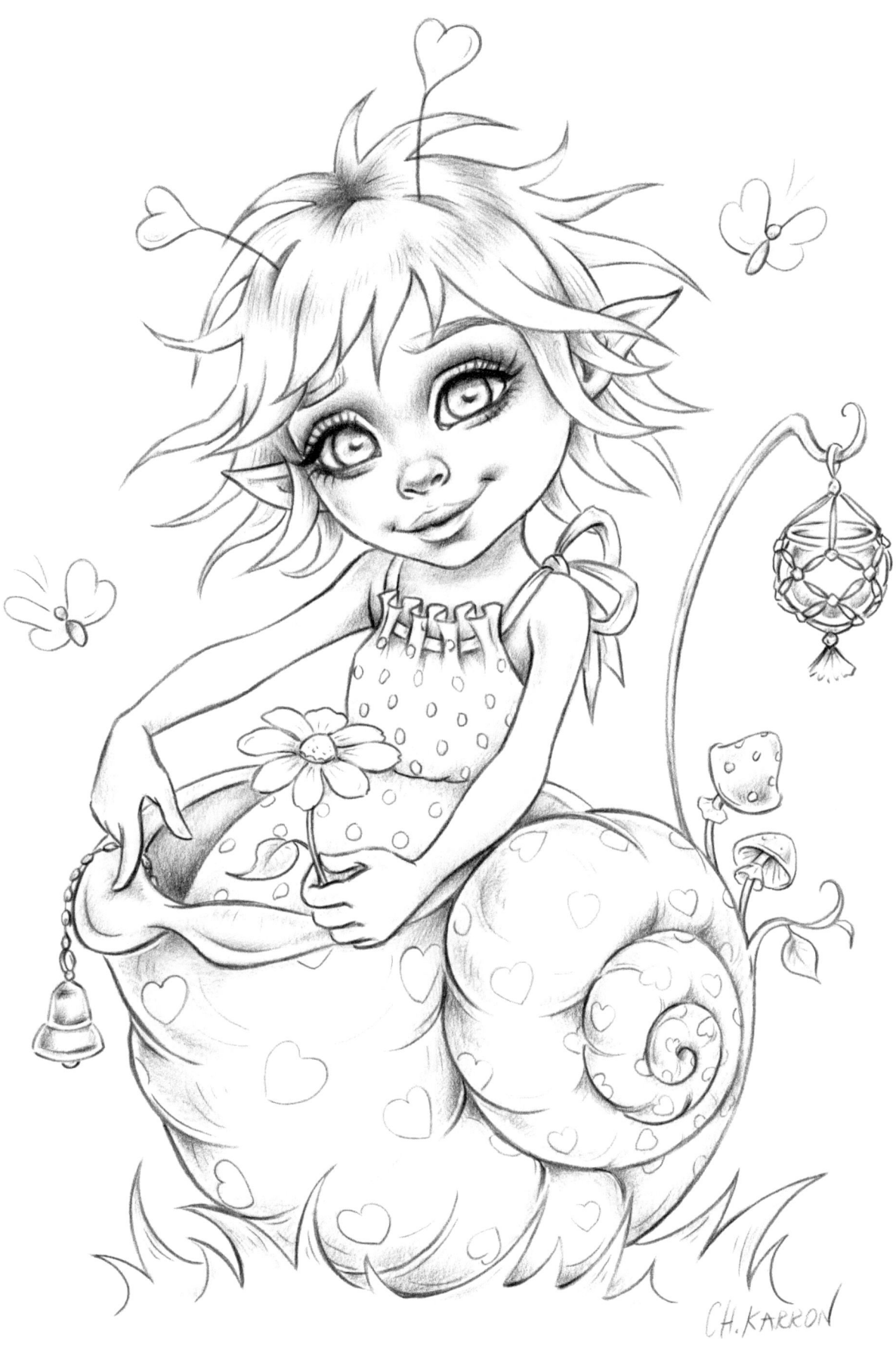

Fairy and Fantasy 5 © Christine Karron

Snail Elfling

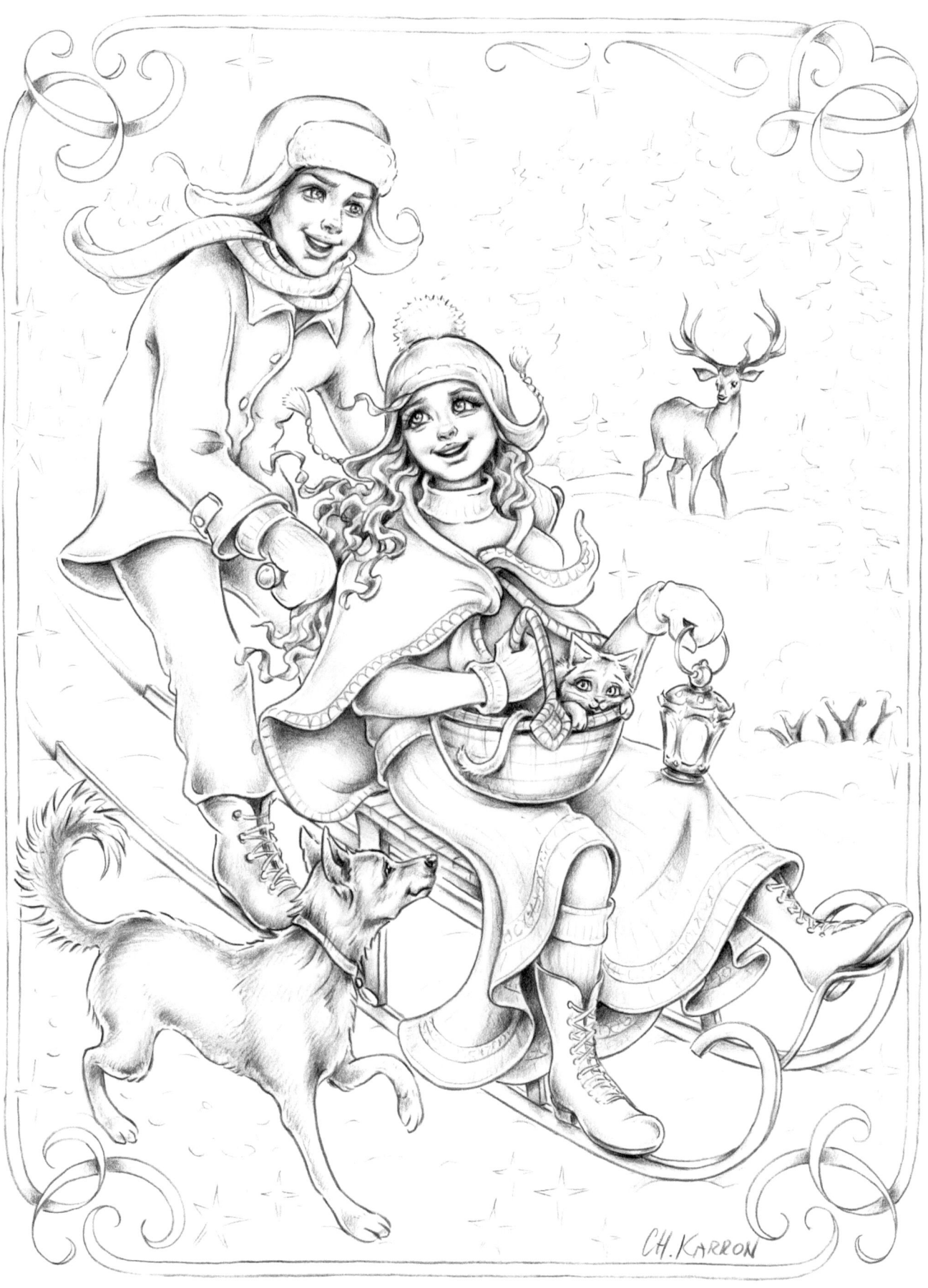

Fairy and Fantasy 5 © Christine Karron

Snowy Trail

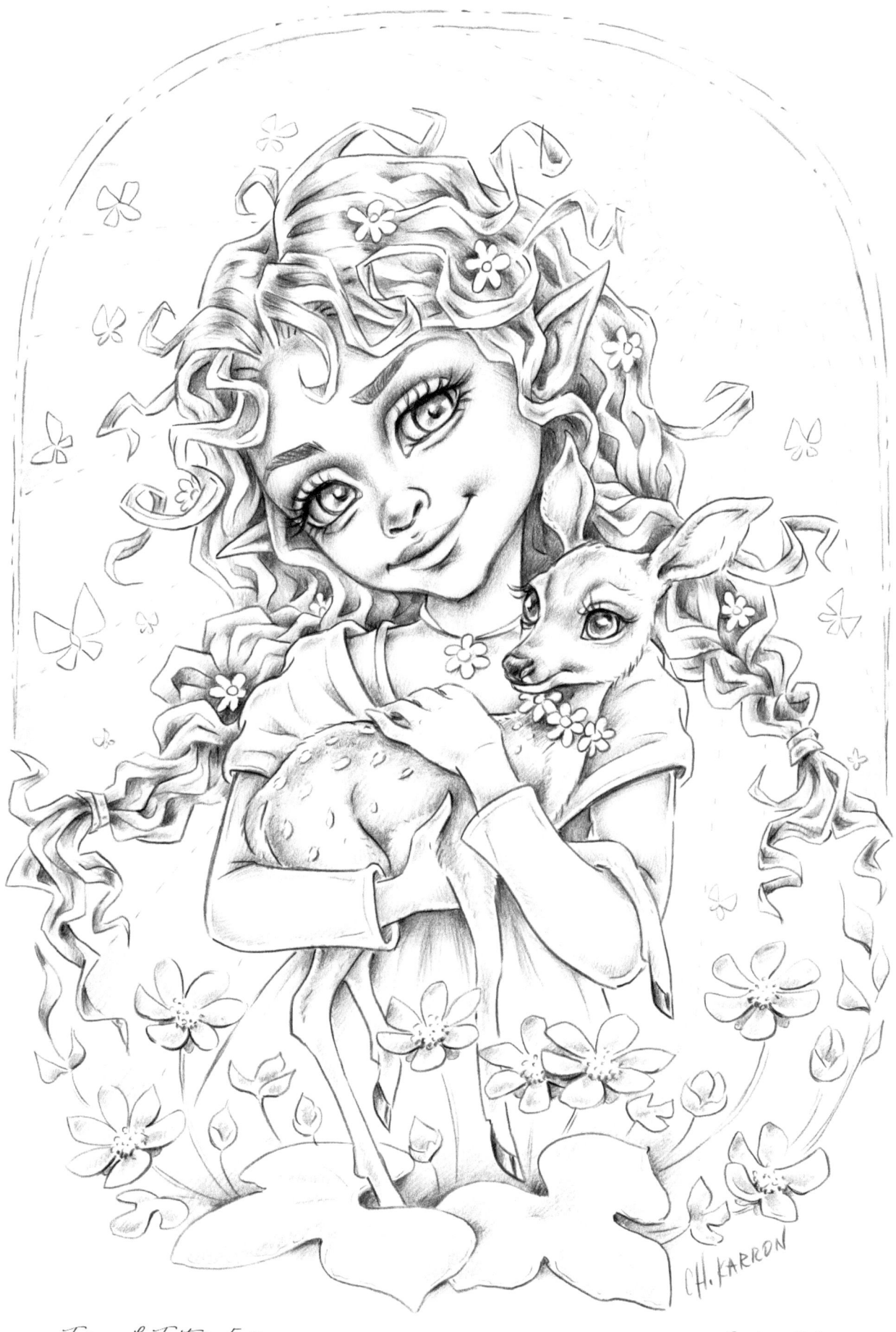

Fairy and Fantasy 5 © Christine Karron

Spring Bringer

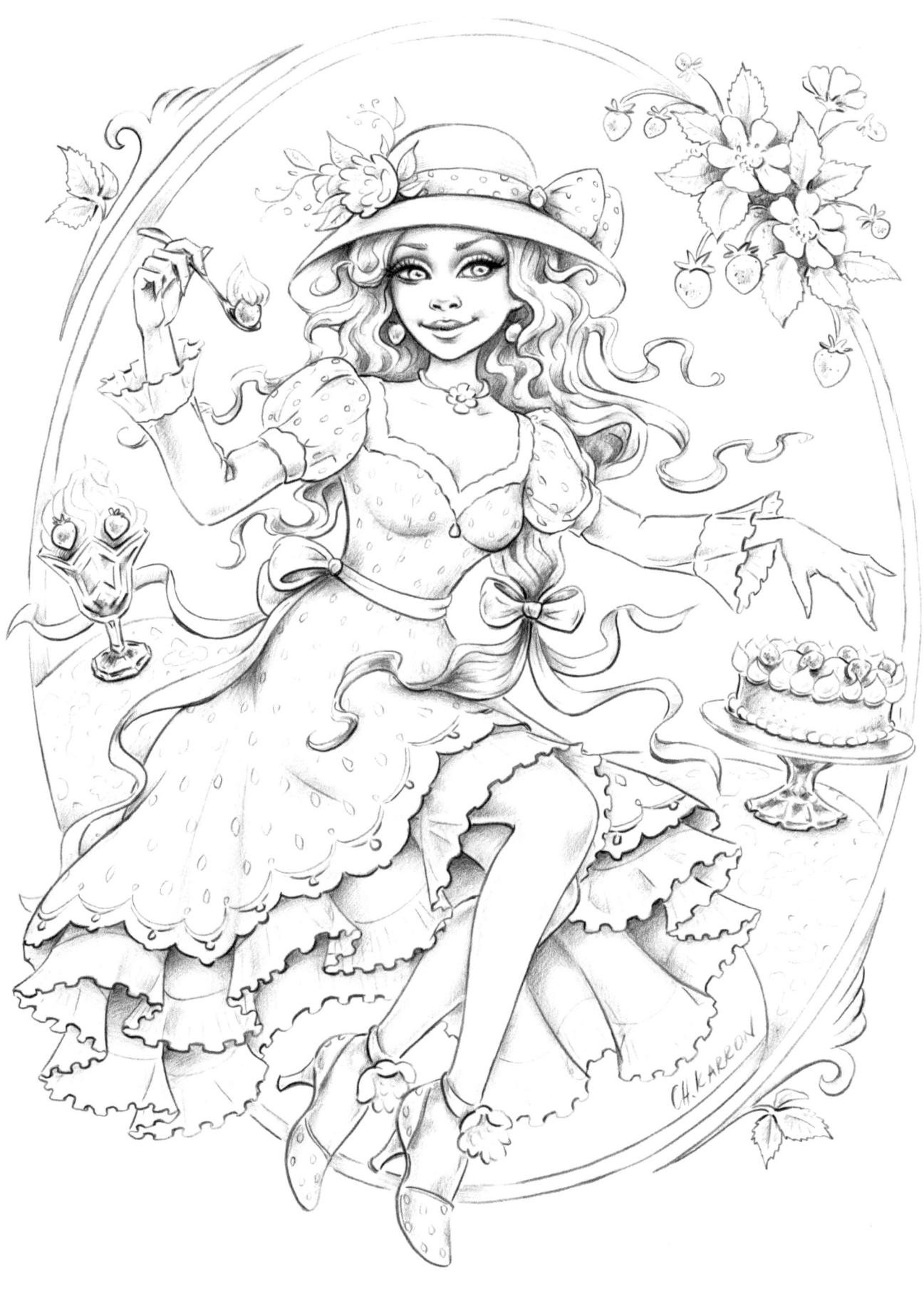

Strawberry Dream

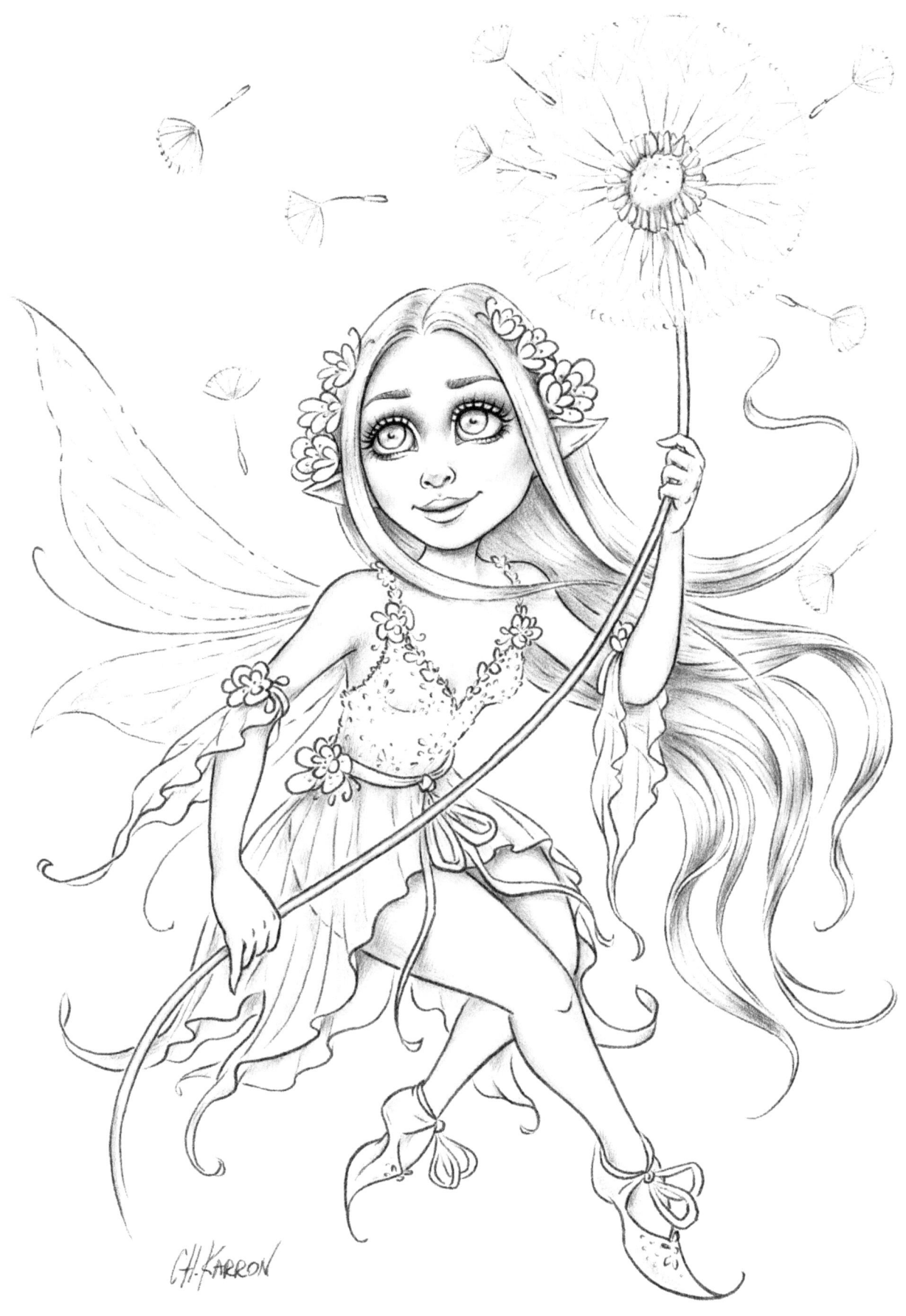

Summer Breeze

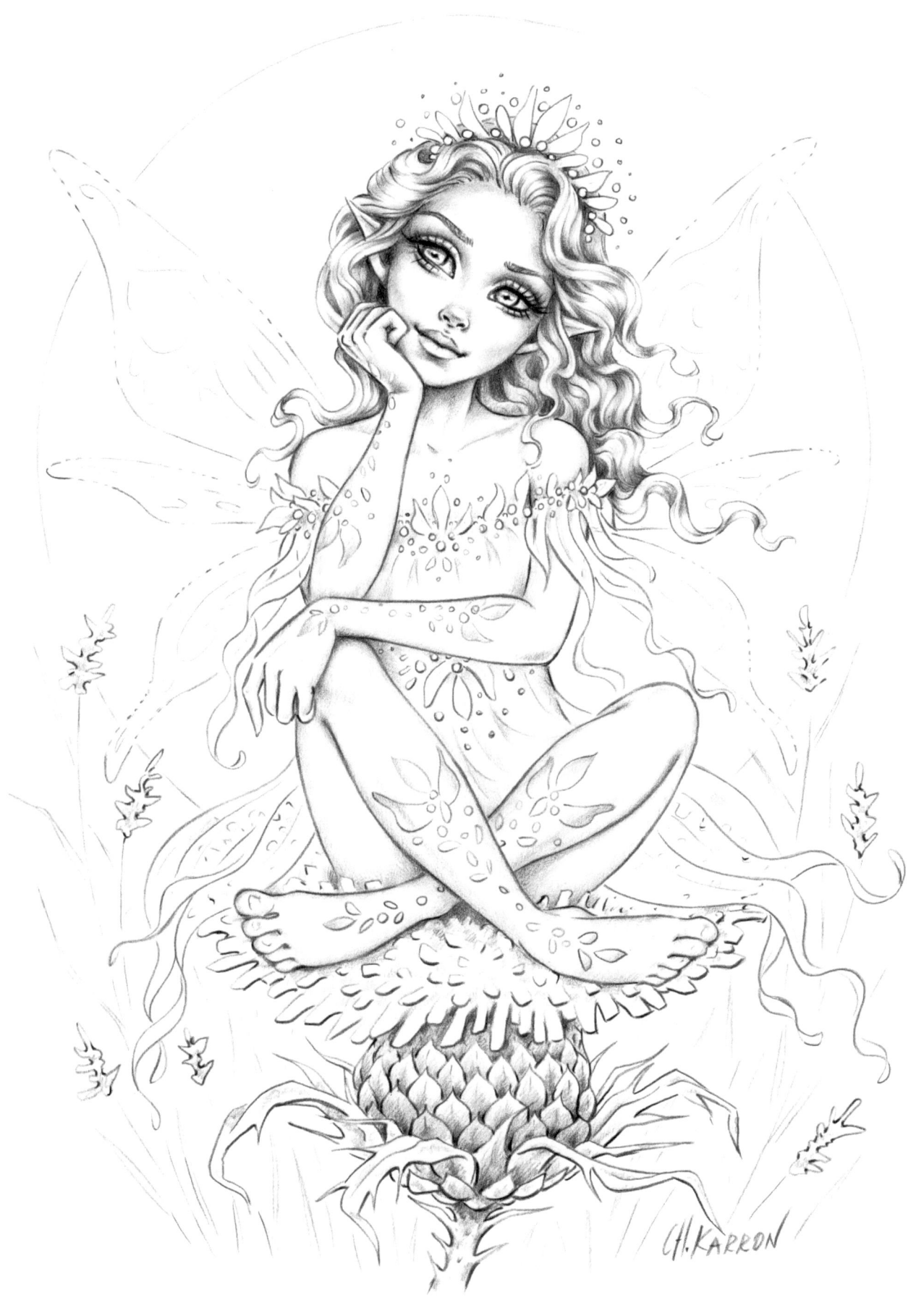

Thistle Landing

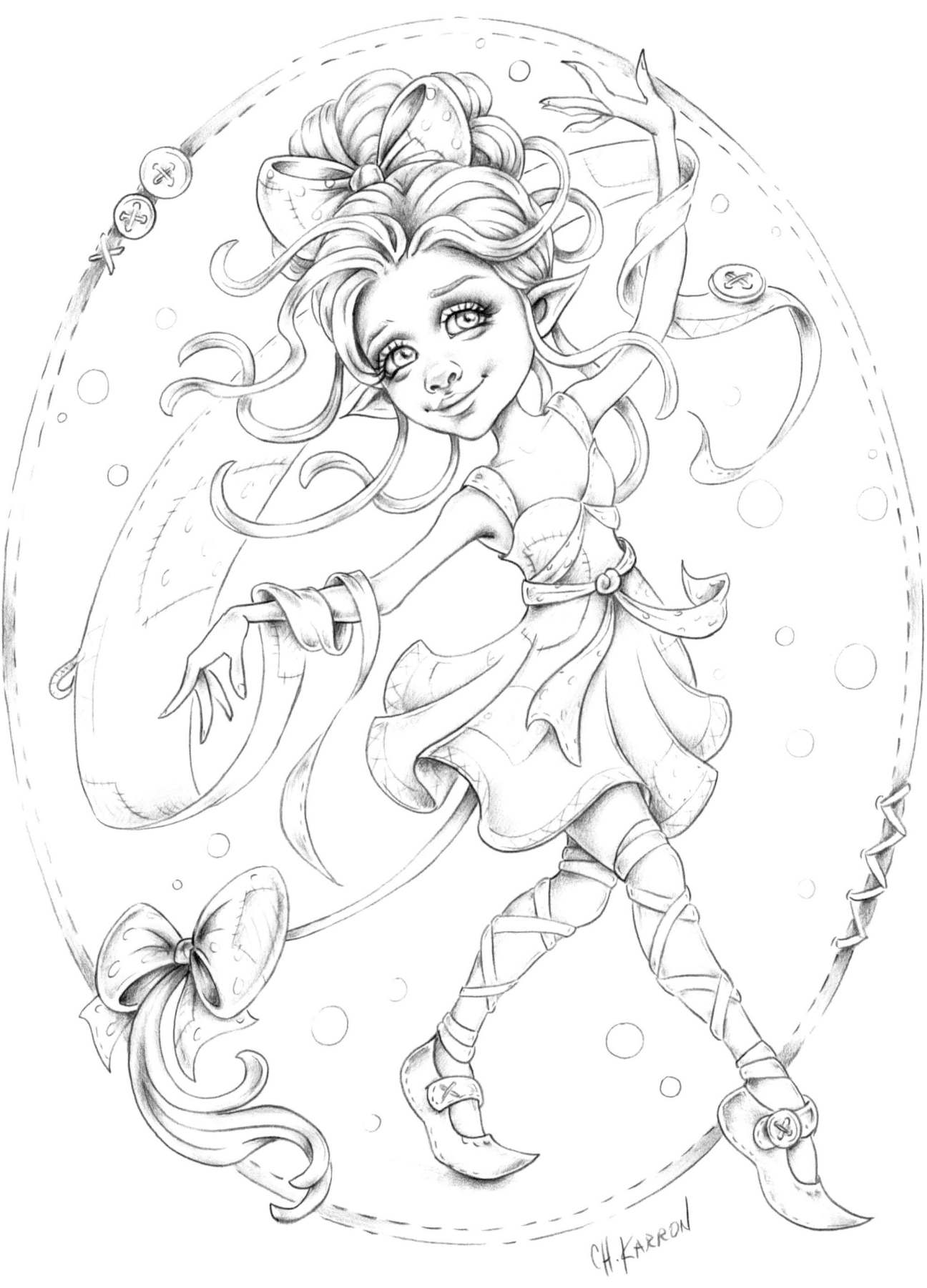

Trollerina

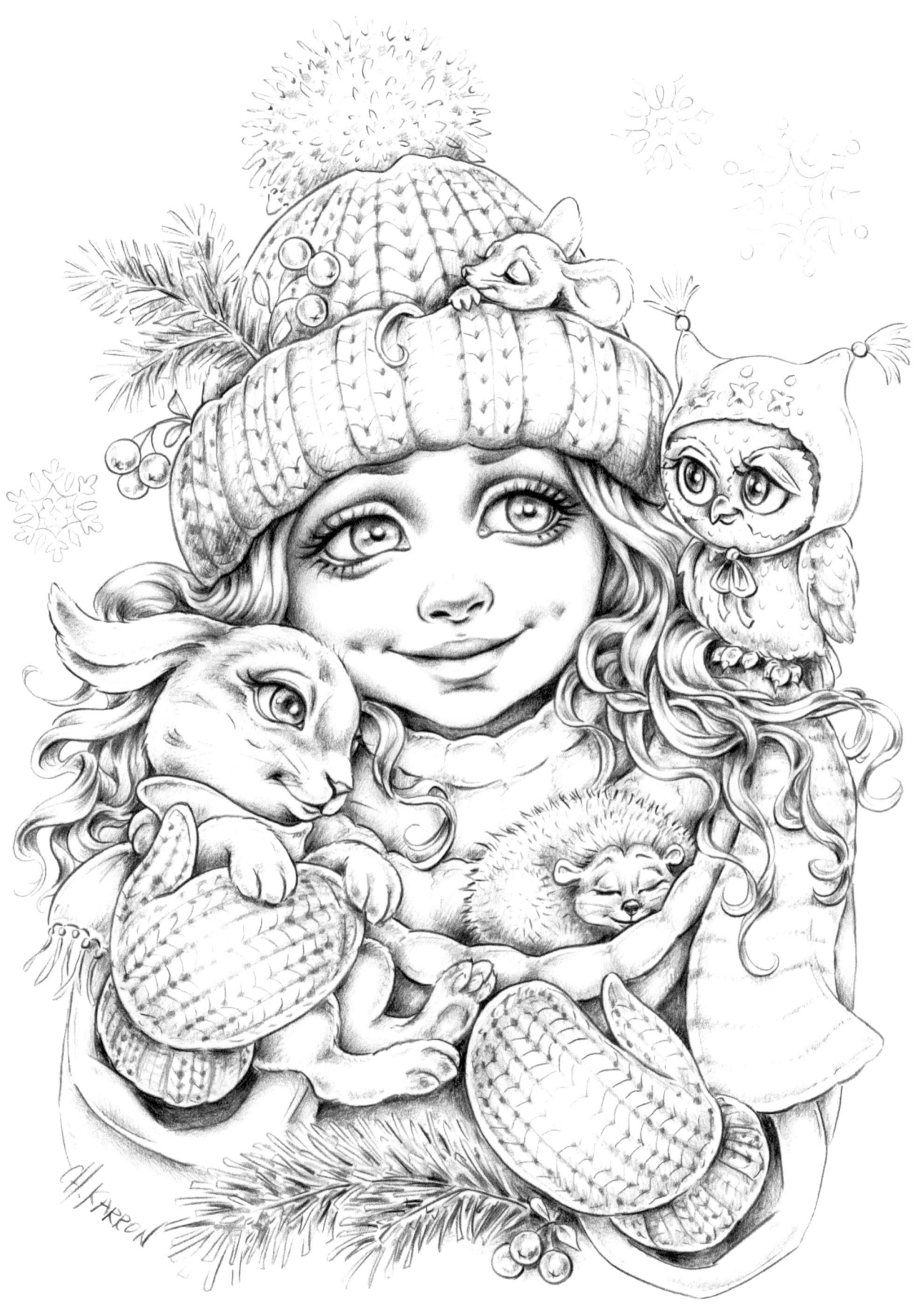

Winter Warmth

Also available:

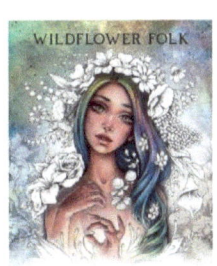
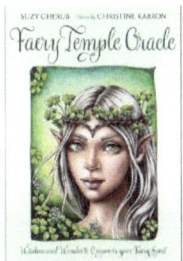
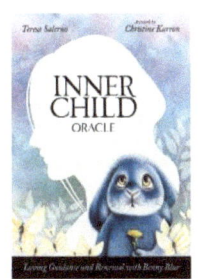
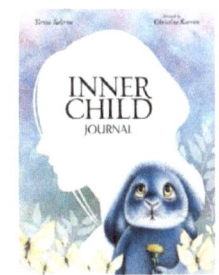

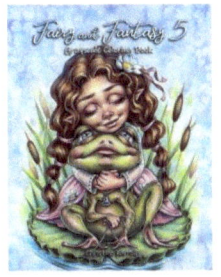
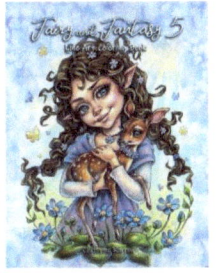
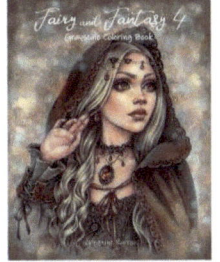
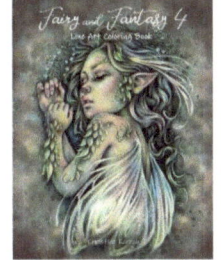
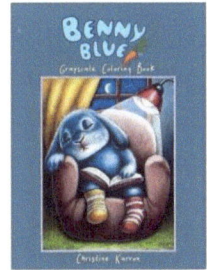

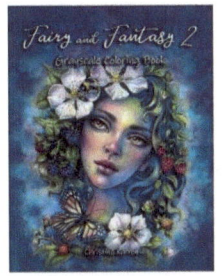
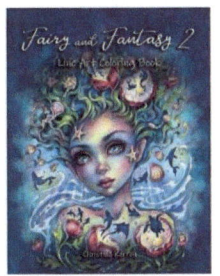
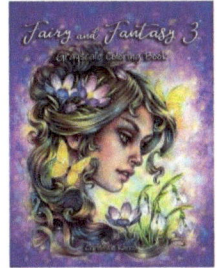
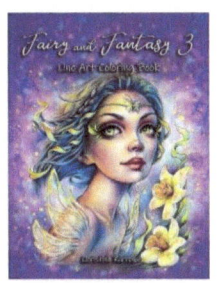
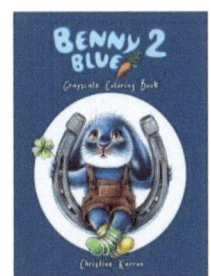

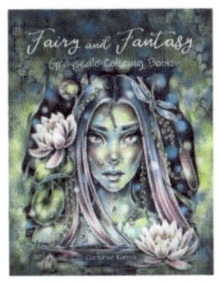
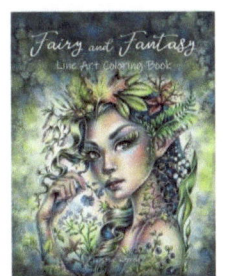
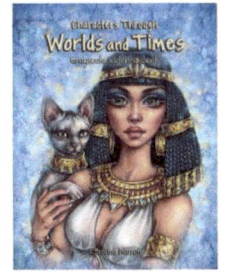
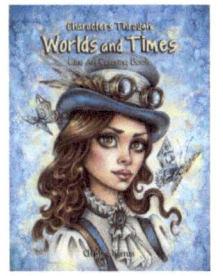
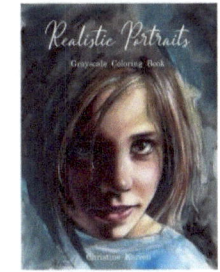

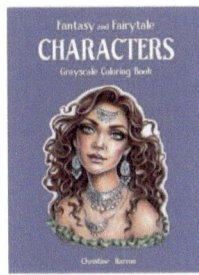
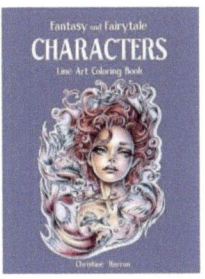
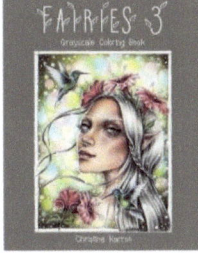
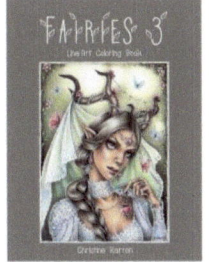
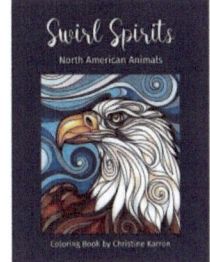

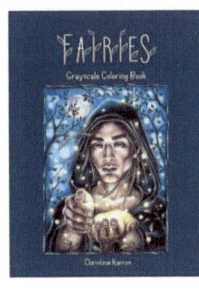
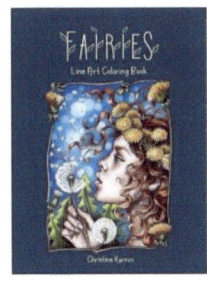
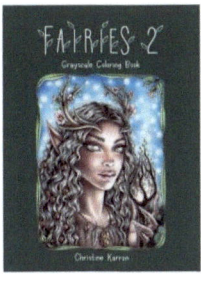
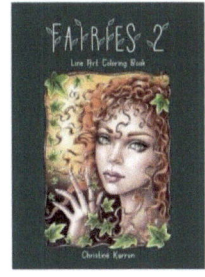
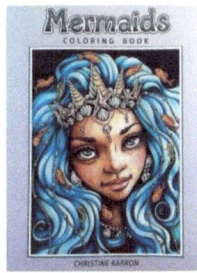

Printable digital coloring page downloads on Etsy:
https://www.etsy.com/shop/ChristineKarron

YouTube videos:
https://www.youtube.com/@chkarron

Instagram: @chkarron
https://www.instagram.com/chkarron

Christine Karron Art and illustration
https://www.facebook.com/chkarron

Christine Karron Coloring Collection Fan Group
https://www.facebook.com/groups/ChristineKarronCCFG

#christinekarron
#chkarron

www.chkarron.com

www.ingramcontent.com/pod-product-compliance
Lightning Source LLC
Chambersburg PA
CBHW041509280526
45792CB00004B/1191